Shine Like a Crystal

12 Quick Tips to Rock Life

Brenda DeHaan

DeHaan, Brenda
Shine Like a Crystal: 12 Quick Tips to Rock Life

ABOUT THIS BOOK

Life is tricky sometimes. It can be as hard as rock, or it can be as shiny and beautiful as a crystal. Since a crystal *is* a rock, it depends on what is happening and how you view your life.

This book has 12 tips with cool photos of rocks (also known as crystals) to show how you can make your life shine most of the time. It all starts with you! You will learn advice about life and will also learn different kinds of rocks. It's a rockin' combo!

Are you ready? (Of course, you are!)

TIP ONE

No matter what someone looks like, always be kind. If you don't know what to say, a smile may say it all.

See how many people you can make smile each day by smiling at them first. *Ready, set, smile!*

Stones pictured are shiva eye shells (eyes), leopard skin jasper (nose), and rhodonite (smile) on selenite slab (face).

TIP TWO

Nobody likes making mistakes. Nobody! Everybody makes mistakes. Everybody!

Nobody wants sad things to happen. Everybody has sad things happen.

These are all a part of life. Learning from them makes us stronger and smarter. These types of lessons are not fun, but you *will* make it through them one day at a time.

When things seem dark, look for some brightness. Sometimes it takes a while, but don't give up. It might be something little, but it's still better than nothing. Sure, things could always be better, but they could also be worse.

Focus on the light as you make your way through the darkness.

A large clear quartz cluster
was made into a lamp.

TIP THREE

Branch out, learn new things, and visit new places. See other landscapes and see how other people do things.

Many times there are many different ways to do many different things. One choice might be right for one person, but a different way may work better for someone else. It's all good!

Dendritic jasper gets the natural fern
designs from iron and manganese filling
the rock's cracks. It's nature's artwork.

TIP FOUR

Do not worry about what other people think. Believe in yourself and love yourself. Your opinion of yourself is the one that matters. Feel comfortable with yourself.

Not only are you enough, you are *more* than enough! Your goodness overflows! You might not realize how special you are, but you really *are* that special!

You have a heart of gold, so glow and let it show!

Pyrite's nickname is "fool's gold,"
but it has a genuine shine.

TIP FIVE

Do not compare. It's not fair. Each person is unique and one-of-a-kind. Enjoy differences. The world would be boring if everyone looked and acted the same. How would you tell each other apart?

With billions of people in the world, we have billions of individuals, each one different. That is how it is supposed to be.

Standing on selenite are angels carved
from six different stones: unakite,
angelite, rainbow fluorite and amethyst
in the back with rose quartz
and tiger's eye in the front.

TIP SIX

Stay positive. Say *no* to negative thinking and negative people. Say *yes* to good ideas and healthy choices. Regrets are not fun, so make your decisions good ones!

Y = lapis lazuli

E = pyrite

S = 3 Indigo Gabbros and 1 amethyst

TIP SEVEN

Listen to others. It makes them feel important. Also, listeners learn a lot.

Even more importantly, listen to yourself and make the best choices for your life. Deep down, you know what you should do. Listen to that inner voice!

The bunny is carved tiger's eye;
the kitty head is a mystery rock found
outside and decorated by a six-year-old.

TIP EIGHT

Enjoy nature and help keep the earth clean. If you see trash on the ground, please pick it up, and throw it away. You are going to be living on this earth for many more decades, so do your best to keep your surroundings clean. Each person's efforts add up to improve the earth.

Doing something little is better than doing nothing at all.

The round stone is Labradorite with azurite and malachite in the background. They are resting on selenite.

TIP NINE

Help others. When you help them, you also are helping yourself feel good. It's win-win!

The turtle was carved from malachite;
the bear was carved from onyx.

TIP TEN

Think! Think before you talk. Think before you act. Take deep breaths through your nose while you think.

Stay calm. Others will listen better if you stay calm. They won't take you seriously if you seem out-of-control.

One way to calm yourself is to breathe out **3** times longer than you breathe in. For example, if you breathe in for a count of 6, breathe out for a count of 18. If you breathe in for a count of 7, breathe out for a count of 21. Try it now and see what you think!

The three hearts were carved from
Labradorite.

TIP ELEVEN

Stick up for other people, and stick up for yourself. Remember to stay calm, logical, and balanced while doing this. Your tone of voice helps to set the tone of the discussion. Yelling makes things worse, not better.

It can be scary defending yourself and others, but it can make a big difference. One person can be the one to make the situation better. Be the one who stands up and stands out.

These fluorite have octahedron
shapes with 8 sides.
Which one stands out to you?

TIP TWELVE

Be natural and be real. Let people see the **real** you, that special person deep down inside. The real you is WONDERFUL—and don't you forget it!

You are not perfect. Nobody is; nobody ever will be.

It is the "flaws" in crystals that cause the light to reflect in rainbow colors. Accept yourself, flaws and all, and shine like a crystal!

Rainbows reflect from this clear calcite.

About the Author

Brenda DeHaan is a K-12 librarian, rock collector, grandma, and author. She took the pictures of the rocks in this book and has written more books about rocks, her pets, and other topics. She loves to read and hopes that you do also.

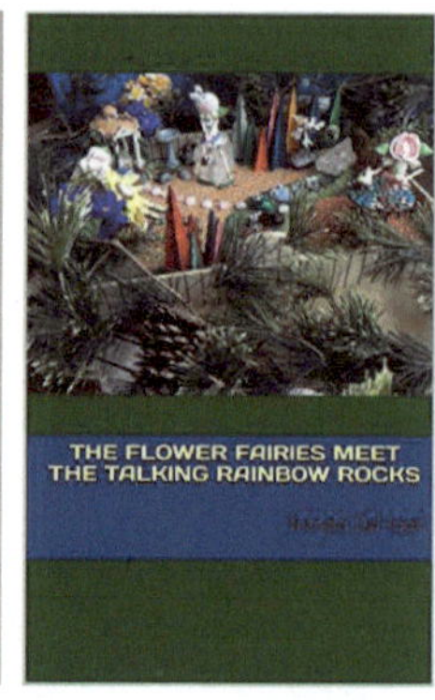

Rocks Rock
Rough and Tumbled, Colorful and Cool Rocks and Minerals
Brenda DeHaan

A B C
Amazing
Book of
Crystals
Fun Photos for
Rock Lovers of All Ages
Brenda DeHaan

LIFE
Advice
for Teens
FROM
AN
AGELESS
GRANDMA
Tips and Encouragement
Just for You
BRENDA DEHAAN